How to Teach in Sunday School: A Guide for Bible Class Teachers

Teaching in the Bible class, Volume 4

Bible Sermons

Published by Guillermo Doris McBride, 2024.

HOW TO TEACH IN SUNDAY SCHOOL: A GUIDE FOR BIBLE CLASS TEACHERS

First edition. April 15, 2024.

Copyright © 2024 Bible Sermons.

ISBN: 979-8224770533

Written by Bible Sermons.

Table of Contents

Children can understand the doctrine of the atoning sacrifice well; it is intended as a gospel for the very young. The gospel of substitution is a simplicity, even though it is a mystery. We must not be content until our little ones know and trust in the finished sacrifice. This is essential knowledge, and it is the key to the other spiritual teachings. Our beloved children must know the cross, and then they will have begun well. Along with all that they receive, they must receive an understanding of this, and then they will have the foundation properly laid.

— Charles Spurgeon

INTRODUCTION

The suggestions contained in this booklet are presented to help believers who, with vocation and dedication, desire greater success in teaching the Word of God. This material is not offered to the reader as an infallible manual or an absolute text for Sunday School instruction; rather, it has been prepared as an elementary guide of orientation for those who want to serve the Lord in this noble ministry.

The author does not claim to be original. Several of the suggestions compiled here are the fruit of the experience of men of God who have left advice to new generations of teachers on the best way to teach youth.

I am sincerely grateful to the brothers and sisters here in Venezuela who, with good will, gave me their valuable help in the preparation of this book. My gratitude also goes to Páginas Orientadoras, from Mexico, who publishes it. Thanks to all of them this little book comes to light.

It is our desire that the content of this work will redound to the glory of God and that the material presented here will be useful to its readers. Let us pray together that these objectives may be achieved in the Lord's will.

1. IMPORTANCE OF THE WORK
Opportunity and necessity

———

Censuses and statistics tell us that in Latin America more than half of the population is under the age of sixteen. This fact represents a great opportunity and at the same time a great responsibility for the believer whose duty and privilege is to teach the Word of God to new generations.

The child learns more easily and more quickly than the adult. The Roman Catholic Church for centuries has declared: Give us a child until he is seven years old and we will have him for life. Communists and fascists make great efforts to indoctrinate the little ones because they know that the children of today are the men of tomorrow. The tender heart of a child is fertile ground for sowing any teaching, be it true or false.

A great part of today's children are not receiving the healthy instruction that is necessary for their moral and spiritual formation for the life ahead of them and for their eternal good. On the contrary, they receive from movies, television, and a multitude of little books with inconsequential, violent and immoral cartoons a pernicious influence that leads them to disaster.

We refer to a case of a child we knew to illustrate the above. A Venezuelan boy named Luis had no father and his mother was forced to work in someone else's house. Luis spent his time watching television at his grandmother's house. One Sunday afternoon the boy jumped from the second floor of a building and hit his head hard. On the way to the aid station Luis told his grandmother how he had seen *Batman* fly on the TV show and was testing to see if he could do the same. His fall caused a brain hemorrhage and shortly after arriving at the hospital emergency room he died.

What a pity that this child did not have the opportunity to attend a Sunday School to hear about God's love and the work of Jesus Christ! If we instruct the children around us with the Holy Scriptures the results could be different.

Jesus Christ and children

The Lord Jesus Christ gave great importance to the little ones. When He walked among men He left precepts and His example regarding the work of teaching them the Word of God:

He thanked God for what He had revealed to the children. 1

He placed a child in the midst of the disciples as an example of humility. 2

He commanded his disciples to let the children come to him. 3

He commanded Peter to feed his lambs. 4

He said that children praise the Lord. 5

He had compassion on the multitudes and began to teach them. 6

If you fail to make the sinner recognize his faults

, Lead the children you can to the benign Savior.

2. REQUIREMENTS FOR TEACHING

For such ministry it is necessary to fulfill the following requirements:

A. Conversion to God

Teaching the things of God is the exclusive privilege of those who have been born again. To be born again means to repent and trust in the Lord Jesus Christ who died for our sins on the cross. The unsaved are spiritually blinded and therefore cannot lead others to the Lord or understand the things of God. Jesus Christ said: If the blind lead the blind, both will fall into the pit. 1 St. Paul wrote to the Corinthians: But the natural man does not perceive the things of the Spirit of God, for they are foolishness to him and he cannot understand them. 2

B. Good testimony

Let us note Paul's advice to Timothy: Be diligent to present yourself approved to God as a workman who does not need to be ashamed. 3 The apostle could also write about how holy, righteous and blamelessly he had conducted himself among the believers. 4 If our life does not support what we teach, our work will be in vain.

C. Sincerity

It is essential that we be sincere and without unworthy motivation. For example, one should not seek to be a teacher in order to show off or to make a good impression on one's peers. Let us strip ourselves of all selfishness. Let us work because the love of Christ constrains us. 5 Everything we do must be done from the heart, as for the Lord and not for men. 6 The sincerity of the teacher will be recognized by the students.

Give the best to the Master, render him faithful devotion

; Let his love so sublime be the motive of every action.

D. Ability to communicate

Ability to teach and stimulate learning are necessary qualities. When you speak without inspiring or motivating your students, you are speaking in vain. It is difficult to communicate what we do not believe wholeheartedly and what does not fill us with enthusiasm. Paul advised Timothy to stir up the fire of God's gift that was in him. 7 It is good for us to receive this advice.

E. Experience

It is customary in some congregations to make new believers responsible for a class when they should be learning in a class that corresponds to their age. In those same churches there may be experienced and knowledgeable brethren who do not have responsibility for a class when they could very well have it.

In some Sunday Schools new teachers first serve as assistants to the more experienced ones. They help by hearing the children say the portions they are learning by heart, designating new texts, keeping order, and teaching the class from time to time. This is a recommended process as long as the teacher is willing to train his assistant and the assistant is willing to learn. Then the assistant can teach the class only when the teacher has to be absent.

F. Dedication to prayer

The sincere teacher feels the need to pray to the Lord:

-For himself, to be a humble, understanding, patient and persistent worker with his class.

-By your message, that the Lord may give you spiritual light. If you do not grieve the Spirit, He can guide you into all truth. 8

-For his disciples, asking God's help to carry out his purposes of conversion, growth in grace, consecration to the Lord and to his service, etc. It is necessary to pray for each one in particular because the effective prayer of the just can do much.9

G. Diligence

As teachers we have to study carefully:

1. Our message. It is necessary to search the Scriptures and prepare the lesson until our own soul is moved. The apostle advised Timothy: Occupy yourself with reading. 10

2. Our students. It is necessary to observe the habits, desires, capacities and homes of each one of them.

Our teaching methods. These must be interesting and effective. Even the most successful method wears out with time. The diligent teacher never stops learning and always seeks the methods that will be of most benefit to his students.

H. Liability

Punctuality: We suggest that the teacher arrives at least ten minutes before class if he/she is not busy transporting students. This way he/she will be able to keep the classroom and teaching materials in order and greet students as they arrive.

Compliance: On occasion when absences are necessary, the teacher in charge seeks a substitute and notifies the superintendent in advance.

I. Sacrifice

A spirit of sacrifice suits us. Our service requires dedication of time, effort in prayer and study, and a willingness to sacrifice our savings for the sake of the boys. Love is measured by sacrifice. Christ loved the church and gave himself for it. 11 The teacher who loves his class will carry them in his heart and will be willing to sacrifice himself to win them to Christ and lead them in the ways of the Lord.

Let us see the necessity of devoting our whole mind to the preparation; devoting our whole soul to the presentation; and devoting our whole life to the illustration of the lesson.

May all my time be consecrated to your praise,

May my lips speak only of your love.

3. THE STUDENT

We teachers should not lose sight of the fact that children, in the process of development, go through periods of transition that profoundly affect their behavior. If we want our teaching to be effective, let us consider the age of our students and be aware of the inclinations of the period they are going through.

A. The first period of childhood (between 3-8 years of age)

The following is characteristic of toddler behavior:

Curiosity. The child has a natural curiosity and an active imagination. We can capture their attention by arousing their curiosity and then maintain it by appealing to their imagination.

Restlessness. Young children are used to activity and it is difficult for them to sit still for an hour. It is advisable to vary classroom activities in order to avoid monotony and allow them movement.

3. Credulity. Since children are willing to believe everything they are told, let us be careful to present them only with truth, and in a way that they can retain it.

4. Sensitivity and sense of guilt. We must remember that every child has a conscience, that he still has a tender heart and that after doing wrong he deeply feels his guilt. Fear can provoke in the child the desire to be forgiven.

5. Longing to be loved and accepted. The spiritual part that God has placed in the child makes him feel fear and guilt and is able to know God's forgiveness. There is in every child, even in the spoiled one, the longing to be loved and appreciated.

The world lacks understanding and true love. Many parents abandon their families. There are mothers without natural affection and people who practice teaching without vocation or true interest in the welfare of the children in their classes. We, the Sunday School teachers, have the duty to show the pupil our love for him. We will do this by speaking of God's infinite love, sending his own Son who bore the punishment so that the child would be forgiven. Our desire is that the child, with sincere faith, will receive the salvation that God offers him. Then we will be able to show him that he is made acceptable in the Beloved. 1

The little ones can turn from

sin And give themselves to Christ who calls them with love;

They can turn from the ways of this world

To walk in the footsteps of their Savior.

B. The final period of childhood (9-12 years)

Let's note some outstanding things about the child at this stage of his life.

1. Awakening of the mind and own criteria. The child is now thinking about life situations, evaluating and making decisions according to his or her own judgment. For this reason, this is the best period to instill in the child the basic truths about sin, responsibility, divine justice, the love of God and the work of Christ.

Spontaneous grouping. The desire to belong to a group manifests itself and sometimes results in problems. Among the effects produced by these groupings are uneasiness, enmity, mockery and hostility. The opinions of the gang exert a great deal of influence on some children.

3. Sense of loyalty. The desire to be loyal to the group can be used to lead the child to understand that the loyalty that is really worthwhile is the loyalty that can be felt toward the Lord Jesus.

Hero worship. Another natural characteristic of children of this age is the admiration they feel for television and movie characters, athletes and the heroes of the books they read. Let's try to use these natural tendencies of the child to interest him/her in the heroes of the faith: men and women who pleased God.

C. The adolescent period (12-18 years)

Characteristic traits of the adolescent:

1. Is in transition. Sometimes acts and thinks like an adult and sometimes like a child.

2. It has unsuspected potential. Today's youth can be tomorrow's leader.

3. Lacks experience. Despite his ability, the adolescent needs some control because he often lacks self-control.

4. Desire fun and joy. Solomon speaks of the natural inclinations of youth: Rejoice, young man, in your youth. 2

5. He is more interested in what he himself does, says or does. When he is forced to be passive and limit himself to listening to the teacher, he often feels frustrated, especially if he does not feel sympathy for his teacher and rebels against the Sunday school. When there is a rebellious attitude it is difficult to achieve good results in his heart.

6. He wants to know. Although at times the young person questions the truths he has been taught, deep down he has a desire to know with certainty what he now begins to doubt. That is why the young person may be attracted to the person who has the answer he is looking for and knows how to give it.

7. Try not to think about the future. It is natural for the young man to concern himself only with the present. The preacher warned: But know that God will judge you on all these things. 3 The teacher, remembering the tendency not to think about the future, should frequently emphasize that youth is a time to prepare and lay a foundation for the future.

8. He needs God. Solomon's advice is still valid: Remember thy Creator in the days of thy youth, before the evil days come, and the years come, when thou shalt say, I have no delight in them. 4

The adolescent is in transition, he is often driven by his emotions. We must understand this. If we want to be instruments in the hands of the Holy Spirit we must learn to work with the young person and not against him.

4. TEACHING GUIDELINES
The purpose of teaching

Jesus Christ is in all the Scriptures. On the morning of the resurrection day he began at Moses, and continuing through all the prophets, he declared to them in all the Scriptures what they said about him. 1

The Sunday School teacher has the duty to present Christ even when studying Old Testament stories with his class. To demonstrate the importance of this we will relate a story taken from real life.

Carlos wanted to attend Sunday School but his father would not give him permission. However, on three occasions when his father was absent, he attended the class with a classmate. Later Carlos became seriously ill and when he was visited in the hospital by an evangelical lady, she asked him if he had ever attended Sunday School.

-Yes," he answered, "I went three times.

-Did you learn anything from the Lord Jesus?

-No ma'am, the first Sunday the teacher talked about Abraham, the second about Joseph and the third she told us the story of Moses, but she didn't get to Jesus.

The lady, thinking of the boy's delicate state, told him about Abraham, and the occasion when God provided a substitute for Isaac. 2 She explained how Jesus Christ was our substitute when He bore our sins in His body on the tree. Next he spoke of how Joseph is an illustration of the Lord Jesus Christ: loved by his father, despised and sold by his brothers, and how he became a preserver of life. 3 Later he spoke of Moses and the bronze serpent. He taught that as Moses lifted up the serpent, so Christ was lifted up on a cross. 4 Charles came to understand that Jesus Christ died for him and there in the hospital he accepted Him as his Savior.

The Bible is the revelation of a person: our Lord Jesus Christ. It is the exposition of a theme: redemption by his blood. We find this in the history, the prophecies, the symbols, the furniture of the tabernacle, 5 and in the whole Bible.

The Bible reveals Christ, the law gives us shadows of him;

Prophets his death said, the psalms also, like a garden.

A. What can we teach young children?

Young children, as we said in the previous chapter, are curious, restless, ready to believe, sensitive and long to be loved. They are drawn to the stories of the Lord Jesus. They like to hear about God's power in creation and about people like Joseph, Moses, Samuel, David, etc. It is good to remember that the toddler retains many of the things he sees, even more of the things he does, but very little of what he just hears.

B. What can we teach older children?

Our goal should be to teach all the major stories of God's Word. If we teach fifty lessons in the course of one year, we can achieve this goal in about five years. We can teach the Old Testament for six months and the New Testament for the remaining months. The following year we pick up where we left off teaching. If the class changes teachers, the new one will start teaching where the other one left off. In this way the students will have knowledge of the Bible stories in their chronological order.

This plan will seem too difficult for the teacher who limits himself to one or two favorite books or who prefers to talk for a long time about a single character or a single chapter. The teacher should not be afraid or lazy in the face of a plan that will help him to broaden his own knowledge of the Scriptures. If the teacher does not study to grow, he and his students are the losers.

Some congregations have the custom of interrupting the systematic teaching of the Sunday School to hold special meetings where a brother gives a message to the entire Sunday School. This can be useful at the beginning or end of a cycle of studies, on dates when the children move from one class to another, but it should not be done very often. Usually the child learns little in these meetings because the teachings do not follow a definite plan, because he loses personal contact with his own teacher, and because the message addressed to all cannot meet the particular needs of each stage of growth.

C. What can we teach teenagers?

Here are some suggestions for topics that might be helpful for students in this age group.

1. Doctrinal themes illustrated by Old Testament stories.

a) The condemnation of man (disobedience of Adam and Eve). 6

b) God's judgment (Sodom and Gomorrah). 7

c) Substitution (the sacrifice of Isaac). 8

d) The decision (Rebeca). 9

e) Reconciliation (Joseph and his brothers). 10

f) Redemption by blood (the Exodus lamb). 11

g) The atonement for sin (the two goats). 12

h) Salvation by faith (the bronze serpent). 13

i) Security (the red cordon). 14

j) Regeneration (dry bones). 15

2. Women of the Bible

The students will have a special interest in the women of the Scriptures. Each girl in the class can prepare and present a report on a woman of the Bible, telling how she pleased or displeased God. These reports can serve as an introduction to the lessons on these women.

3. Young guerrillas

For the "activist" spirit in the young man, there are biographies of characters such as Jephthah, Gideon, David and Jonathan.

4. The two natures of the believer

It is advisable to teach that the believer has two natures and that there is constant conflict between the new man (the spirit) 16 and the old man (the flesh). 17

The coming of the Lord Jesus Christ

The truth of the second coming of the Lord 18 and other future events such as the judgment seat of Christ 19 has awakened in many young people the desire to be saved and to use their lives for the glory of God. In order to teach these truths in a convincing way we must live in expectation of the coming of our Master and Lord.

Speak to me, O Lord, and I will speak in living echoes of your voice;

And, as thy found one, I will seek the lost for God.

JESUS CHRIST, THE GREAT TEACHER

One is your Teacher, the Christ." 1 "What teacher is like him? "2 "And when he came into his own country, he taught them in their synagogue, so that they marveled, and said, Whence hath this man this wisdom and these miracles? "3 "Never man spake like this man!"4

The incomparable Master taught the divine truths in many ways: by living holy, working miracles, using examples, making comparisons, asking questions, telling parables, etc. Let us contemplate him in action:

A. Your example

God esteems works of greater importance than words. That is why Luke wrote: These are the things which Jesus began to do and to teach, 5 and said that Christ was mighty in deed and word. 6 Let us notice the order of things in these two quotations.

Our deeds during the week speak louder than our words on Sunday. It is God whom we must please before men. The verse quoted states that Jesus was mighty in deed before God first, and then before all the people. Our Sunday School service should be done in such a way that the Lord is glorified first; if so the students will be benefited.

B. His miracles

Jesus of Nazareth was a man approved by God with wonders, wonders and signs. 7 The apostle John, for example, relates seven of his miracles or signs in the first eleven chapters of his Gospel. Sometimes one evangelist adds details that the other does not mention. Each evangelist highlights in his account the details that bring out the focus with which he presents the person of the Lord Jesus Christ.

The miracles testify to the divinity of Christ always bring teachings regarding the weakness of the human being in contrast to the power of God. Jesus Christ is still a miracle worker because He has all power in heaven and on earth. He changes sorrow into joy, spiritual darkness into light and sinners into saints.

C. Your object lessons and comparisons

God used many objects to attract the attention of the people of Israel. The prophets used, for example, the mason's plummet, [7] good and bad figs, [8] the rod of an almond tree, [9] a rotten girdle, [10] etc. The evangelists likewise relate that Jesus spoke of a coin, [11] of birds, [12] of the lilies of the field, [13] etc. He took a child and taught the necessity of humility; [14] he took a towel and with it taught the importance of service; [15] with the loaves he taught the security of divine provision. [16]

The Lord's language was rich in easy-to-understand comparisons. He called the false prophets wolves in sheep's clothing; [17] their death was compared to a grain of wheat dying in the ground; [18] the hypocrites he called whited sepulchres; [18] he compared rebirth by the Holy Spirit to the wind. [20]

D. Your questions

The Lord often asked questions. He did not do so out of ignorance, nor to tempt, but because he wished to involve his listeners in the conversation, making them reflect. For example: Who do men say that the Son of Man is? 21 Is it lawful on the sabbath days to do good? 22 What thinkest thou, Simon? 23 Who of these three seemeth to be the neighbor? 24

E. His parables

A biblical parable is not a story, but a comparison taken from common life in the form of a plausible account. God said in Hosea: Through the prophets I used parables. 25 Jotham told the parable of the trees. 26 Nathan told David about the rich man who killed the poor man's sheep, so that David would recognize his sin. 27

Jesus Christ spoke in parables and the people listened to him willingly. 28 The Gospels contain about fifty of his parables. The parable of the prodigal son 29 is easily read in three minutes and is one of the longest. They deal with such subjects as lost things, 30 the boys in the market place, 31 the robbed traveler, 32 the wedding garment, 33 etc. By means of parables Christ taught divine truths.

F. Your words

Nicodemus called the Lord Jesus *Master*. 34 Well did the Lord know that this man had his own ideas, but He did not waste time talking about them but warned him at once about the necessity of being born again. We should speak the words that Christ spoke, whether they refer to Himself or to the sinner. Christ said: The words that I have spoken to you are spirit and they are truth. 35

More of Jesus I want to learn, more of his grace to know,

More of his gifts to receive, more with others to share.

6. TEACHER PREPARATION

We cannot count on the Lord's help if we do not take time to study His Word. In the Bible we notice that God always calls to his service people who are busy doing something. In the difficult times of the judges there was a man named Gideon, who shook the wheat in a winepress. Shaking the wheat can speak to us of studying the Scriptures seeking spiritual food. God watched him and we read that the angel of the LORD appeared to him and said, The LORD is with thee, thou mighty man of valor. 1

In view of the great importance of Sunday School we should feel our responsibility before the Lord to prepare the lesson in such a way that the Holy Spirit can use it for the blessing of the students, both the unsaved and the saved.

The Lord Jesus said: The children of this age are more shrewd in dealing with their fellow men than the children of light. 2 Unfortunately, this is sometimes very evident in the Sunday School. The government of the country requires that those who teach in the schools study pedagogy and that they have a proper knowledge of the subjects in their charge. However, many believe that Sunday School teachers can impart divine truths to the youth without any preparation.

It is true that God can do His work without the wisdom and preparation of this world, and that the Holy Spirit directs and helps the believer who is in communion with Him, but none of this gives us freedom to neglect our preparation. Let us keep in mind that God declares: Cursed is he that doeth the work of the Lord carelessly. 3

A. Your private study

———

Ezra, the scribe, was one of the most outstanding teachers of the Old Testament. Let us look at his preparation according to Ezra 7:10:

1. Preparation of the heart. "For Ezra had prepared his heart". Above all things kept, keep your heart. 4

2. Preparation of the mind. "For Ezra had prepared his heart to search the law of the LORD." Ezra diligently studied the Word of God. Search the Scriptures. 5

3. Preparation through obedience. "For Ezra had prepared his heart to seek the law of the LORD and to do it ..." What ye have learned and received and heard and seen in me, this do. 6

4. Instruction as a result of preparation. "...and to teach in Israel his statutes and judgments". Paul wrote to Timothy: Occupy yourself with reading and teaching. 7

The work of the Sunday School is the work of the Lord. The apostle wrote: Whatsoever ye do, do it heartily, as to the Lord, and not unto men: for Christ the Lord ye serve. 8

In the book of Ecclesiastes the wise Solomon said: The wiser the preacher (or teacher) was, the more he taught wisdom to the people, and caused them to hear, and caused them to search. The preacher sought to find pleasing words, and to write right words of truth. 9

Open my eyes, O Lord; open my eyes, O Lord;

And I shall see wonders in thy law, if thou wilt teach me, O Lord.

B. Reference books.

God's Word is our guiding text and is self-explanatory. Our best source of teaching material is found in the Scriptures. In addition to the lesson passage, there are often parallel passages. This occurs in the books of Kings and Chronicles and in the four Gospels. By reading these passages together we have the most complete story. The references in the margins of the Bible are helpful in finding these passages and also notes such as those of Dr. Scofield.

The teacher should have a concordance and a Bible dictionary at hand. The concordance will save him a lot of time and will lead him to verses that will be of help to develop the subject he is preparing. There are many commentaries that shed light on the books that make up the Bible but there is a danger in them. Before studying or buying a book written by an unknown author it is advisable to consult with a more knowledgeable brother.

In some evangelical bookstores we can obtain manuals for the use of the teacher and lessons that come with figures for the flannel board. Some of these materials are very helpful. But we suggest that the teacher do his own study of the Scriptures first, jot down his thoughts, and then add what he finds helpful from other books.

Buying books represents an expense for the teacher, but who among us does not spend more on the support of his body than on that of his soul?

C. The teacher's files

———

Without much expense we can collect in our archives material for the lessons we are going to teach. The file is constructed with a large cardboard box and folders made of folded cardboard, each with a title. The infant teacher will keep pictures, drawings and figures. The one who teaches older children or young people will file maps, charts, sketches, preaching and teaching notes he has heard, stories and clippings from magazines, newspapers, tracts, and calendar sheets that serve to illustrate or introduce the lessons. He will also keep in his files photos and articles about places and customs from biblical times and archeological discoveries.

In some adolescent classes it is often difficult to motivate some students who know the lesson to be studied to the point of exhaustion. How can we get their interest in a lesson they think they already know? The teacher of young people should be in constant search of information, filing details, circumstances and customs of biblical times. Then the presentation of this material should be according to the capacity and interest of the students, to help them appreciate more the truths of the gospel and biblical doctrine.

Genesis 11:31 simply says that Abram, Sarai and the others left Ur of the Chaldees for the land of Canaan. What would this move mean for Sarai? Archaeological discoveries show that Ur was a civilized city, with comfortable homes. Abram and Sarai left all that behind as they set out on a journey of about two thousand miles and for the rest of their lives dwelt in tents. They longed for a heavenly city that God had prepared for them. 10

Read the Bible, its beautiful stories bring heavenly health to the soul:

Fill thy spirit with all its glories, and thou shalt enjoy its heavenly light.

7. TEACHING PLANNING

To plan is to establish a work plan in advance. We set an objective, outline the steps we are going to follow and gather the material we are going to use to achieve the proposed objective. This can be done on a long-term or lesson-by-lesson basis. Having a goal inspires confidence. If we map out in advance what we intend to accomplish, we will know how to make plans to reach our goal. This will help us distinguish between what is urgent, what is important and what is essential.

Long-term planning

Having considered in a general way our responsibility as teachers, the needs of the students and the content of our textbook (the Bible), we will be in a position to prepare a long-term plan. In this plan we will write down what we want to teach each Sunday.

We have to take into account the group of students entrusted to us: their ages, their gender, what they have already learned from the Scriptures, their knowledge and experience, and what interests them.

Taking advantage of the interest that some students will have in certain days of the year, we can incorporate new lessons or modify the order of the ones we have already chosen. For example: on Arbor Day a lesson on certain trees in the Scriptures would be interesting; on Mother's Day the lesson could be about the gift that Jesus Christ presented to a mother; 1 in the month of December the children will be especially interested in the story of the birth of Jesus Christ.

The main point is that the plan and the manner in which the teaching is presented must be in accordance with the ability and understanding of the students. The apostle was, humanly speaking, a very intelligent and well-instructed man; nevertheless, he recognized that as a child he spoke, thought and judged as a child. 2

It takes willpower to draw up and carry out a long-term plan; but if we do it in communion with the Lord, He will help us.

A young believer told how she learned how helpful it was to prepare and follow a plan in teaching. This is what she told me:

-I was given a class of twelve to fourteen year old girls and I tried to teach them the Bible stories I knew. At the end of a year I had to admit that I had accomplished very little with them. I asked for the Lord's help and then prepared a series of lessons on the Lord Jesus Christ. We studied Christ as the Messiah who fulfilled the Old Testament prophecies, as the Lamb of God who takes away the sin of the world, we studied Him as the Teacher and various other titles or offices that we find in the Gospels. Finally we came to the last of these lessons, the most solemn: the Lord Jesus Christ as Judge (John 5:22; Revelation 20:11). The following Sunday evening I received a phone call from one of my students and this is what she told me:

-All week I have been thinking about the lesson and asking myself: How will I be able to present myself to the Lord before the Great White Throne? But, Master, I know I will never have to because tonight I received Him as my Savior.

Planning by lesson

Having an archive, as we have already suggested, greatly facilitates planning, since it provides us with the working material that we may require at any given time.

A teacher who has enjoyed blessings in his classroom describes his method in the following words:

I have fifty-two folders, one for each lesson of the year, with the lesson topic and date marked on each. I look for and file notes, maps, charts, and graphic charts that have to do with the theme of each lesson. When I start preparing a certain lesson I first refer to the objectives in the long term planning. Then I review the material in the corresponding folder, evaluating, eliminating and selecting the material I will use.

Planning is the opposite of improvising. Sunday School teaching requires preparation before the Lord, and the earlier in the week we begin, the better. First let us prayerfully ask for the Lord's help; then let us carefully read portions of the Scriptures, taking notes on our personal meditation; then we can consult manuals and other books; then we will determine how to use the materials on file.

Teaching order

There are three types of order that we must take into account in lesson planning:

A. Order of understanding. We will begin our teaching with what the child knows and take him to what he does not yet know. This is the basis of true teaching. We must begin with known experiences, the similarities between the known and the unknown, and then by graduated steps lead the child to new discoveries.

B. Psychological order. The toddler is very limited in his experiences, but this does not mean that he is incapable of thinking. The thinking process (selecting and applying knowledge to a problem) can be developed even in a toddler under the guidance of a good teacher. It is necessary to connect new lessons with those that have already been learned so that the child can transfer what he already knows to the subject of the new lessons.

C. Chronological order. Let us try to give a clear idea of the order in which the events in the Scriptures took place. A study of the seven dispensations, pointing out some important events in each, may be helpful to a class of young people. Such a study makes it clear that history is the unfolding of God's plans and purposes. A complete outline of the dispensations is found in Scofield's Annotated Bible.

Lesson organization

The lesson can be organized as follows:

A. The main theme. The theme of the lesson is the basic truth that the teacher wants to instill in his disciples. In the Bible there are a number of themes that could be selected. We will present some as examples: the fall of man, the promise of a Savior, the Lamb of God.

B. The key text. This text should express the theme of the lesson and help the student to fix his thoughts on that truth. It may be a part of the passage that will be read in class or perhaps another Scripture. For example, if the lesson will be about the fall of man as told in Genesis 3, the key text might be: As by one man sin entered into the world, and death by sin, and so death passed upon all men, for that all have sinned. 3

C. The Scripture passages to be read. It is usually best not to read too much at one time in class, especially if the students are young or restless children, since they do not always understand what is being read or pay attention. But, something from the Word of God should be read each time the teacher meets with his class.

D. Introduction to the lesson. This could be a question, a brief illustration, pictures or drawings, an object to be shown, etc.

E. Portion assigned. The teacher who wants to please his Lord does not randomly choose the verses to be learned by heart. The one who is truly interested in the welfare of his group will think carefully about how much and what to assign as homework. It is our duty to teach the students the textual words of the Bible. The apostle Paul knew the home in which Timothy was brought up and reminded him: From childhood you have known the Holy Scriptures, which are able to make you wise for salvation..... 4 That is, the words he learned as a child would now help him in spiritual things.

It is easier to teach a verse if we divide it into phrases. For example, John 3:16 can be divided in this way, teaching and explaining one phrase before moving on to the next:

-For God so loved the world,

-who has given his only begotten Son,

-so that everyone who believes in him,

-don't get lost,

-but may he have eternal life.

We should not dispense with repetition and review of the Scriptures learned. There are many ways to avoid boredom and maintain interest. We can prepare posters by writing on one side the reference and the complete letter of the verse. On the other side are placed figures and a word or two that will help the student to remember what he has learned.

For example, to remember John 5:24 we can do the following:

-the figure of an ear

-an open Bible

-the word *believes*

-the word *condemnation*, crossed out

-a black square or circle with the word *death*

-another yellow or orange with the word "life".

-an arrow indicating movement from the first to the second.

The teacher must also learn by heart the texts he assigns to his students. The people of Israel were counseled: These words which I command thee this day shall be upon thine heart, and thou shalt teach them to thy children, and shalt talk of them when thou sittest in thine house, and when thou walkest by the way, and when thou liest down, and when thou risest up ... and thou shalt write them upon the doorways of thy house, and upon thy gates. 5

Awards stimulate effort. They are not for homework completed but recognition of the work done by the student. It is preferable to offer an inexpensive reward to each child who learns the assigned portion than something expensive to the one who learned it first. A good reward for the student who is interested in learning the assigned portions would be an attractive text that he could hang on his wall at home.

F. Main points of the lesson. In the plan there will be a list of the points we want to teach and the order in which they are to be taught.

G. Questions about the lesson. We will see below how the questions should be.

H. Illustrations. Illustrations serve to shed light on the lesson. They should be well distributed throughout the lesson without being too many in number. When the lesson is somewhat difficult or we are introducing a new concept it is good to be able to say: -For example-suppose .... Just look at the effect these statements have on the students to see the value of an illustration. Let us notice how many illustrations Christ used in the sermon on the mount. 6

I. Application of the lesson and brief conclusion. Sufficient time should be allowed at the end of the class hour to review the main truth contained in the lesson in order to apply it to the life of each student. The conclusion can take the form of an invitation to accept the Lord

Jesus Christ as Savior or an exhortation regarding the Christian life if the students are already saved. Sometimes the application will be direct; at other times it will be done indirectly by means of questions. In any case it should be brief so that the students take it to heart.

Teach me, Lord, and I will always teach your things in season;

Give me words, and I will reach the tenderhearted.

8. DIFFERENT APPROACHES

We have noted that each lesson should deal with a basic theme or truth from the Scriptures. In this chapter we are going to use the story of the manna in the wilderness (Exodus 16) as a symbolic figure of the Lord Jesus, the Bread of Life. Let's see how the teacher can teach this truth in different ways, according to the capacity and knowledge of his students.

We will use the lesson plan suggested in the previous chapter: define the topic; use a text that expresses the teaching well; decide which Scripture passage we are going to read in class; determine which points we want to explain; think of appropriate questions; prepare illustrations; end with a brief application of the story and the spiritual condition of the students.

We will remember that the divine truth is one, but students are at different levels in their knowledge of the Word of God.

A. Small beginners

The little children, when they begin to attend the class, do not understand what a symbolic figure is, but we can talk to them about the care that God had for his people and that he also has for us. We can tell the story of the Israelites in a simple way, taking Exodus 16:15 as the key text: "This is the bread that the Lord gives you to eat".

It will be necessary to explain that God sent this food day after day for many years, and that everyone had to look for it and eat it. Who sent bread from heaven? Who sends the rain so that the plants grow? Who gives the food to us? God who knows us and loves us is the one who sustains all creation. The Lord Jesus Christ is God the Son. An appropriate hymn for this lesson is: Christ Loves Me, Loves Me.

B. Older children

They will be able to understand that the miraculous provision of bread for the people of Israel speaks of the One who came to supply our spiritual need. Then we can tell them about the Bread of Life in John 6:35, connecting it with Nehemiah 9:15: "You gave them bread from heaven in their famine".

The reading could be limited to a selection of verses from Exodus 16 and then John 6:31-35. In briefly telling the story of the Israelites we would explain that they could not sow because they were in the desert and were wanderers; they were hungry, and God rained down bread from heaven. We would talk about what the manna was like and that the people, when they saw it for the first time on the sand, asked: Man hu, man hu, which means: What is this? Moses answered them: It is the bread that God has given you to eat.

Before asking questions we could illustrate the lesson to make it clear that the manna is a symbolic figure of the Lord Jesus Christ. We eat bread, vegetables, meat and fruits. Why? To sustain life, for the body to grow and for our organism to perform its ordinary functions.

Now comes the application. This is found in John 6:31-35. Jesus Christ is the Bread of Life: he came from heaven, was born of a virgin, grew up, worked miracles, taught people and gave his life to save us and give us eternal life. If we rely on daily bread to sustain physical life, we must rely on the Bread of Life for eternal life. A chorus that expresses this truth is: I am the Bread of Life, saith the Lord.

C. Adolescents

The approach discussed above is appropriate for older students as well, but covering John 6:51 and a slightly longer reading in Exodus 16. The teacher will be able to apply the account in more detail: the manna came from heaven, like Christ; it was small, which speaks of Christ's humility; it was round, like the eternal which has no beginning and no end; it was white, a figure of the purity of the Lord Jesus; it tasted like honey, as Christ is sweet to the one who receives him; it fell on the face of the earth, reminding us that Christ is within reach of all; it had to be gathered in the morning as it melts at sunrise, "Remember thy Creator in the days of thy youth" and "They find me who seek me early" 2; the manna bred worms and stank when not eaten, so knowledge without obedience can produce indifference and pride.

The teacher will have read Numbers chapter 11 at home, but probably will not want so much reading in a class of this age. But he may add that the manna was transparent like the bedelion, symbol of the blameless life of the Lord Jesus Christ; it was cooked, as the Lord suffered the heat of God's wrath; it tasted like new oil, as the sacrifice of Christ is always fresh to those who trust in him; it fell on the dew and had no contact with the earth, as the Lord was not contaminated by the world.

Questions can begin with why the manna and where it came from. If the family didn't have time to pick it up in the morning, could they pick it up later in the day, why not, when should we receive Christ, and is anything lost by receiving Christ while young?

The soldiers under the orders of Bolivar, Paez and Sucre often had swollen feet when walking long distances and not infrequently suffered hunger. The Israelites, however, walked for forty years and their feet did not swell, and they did not need anything. 3 The manna was food for them. He who eats of the Bread of Life has eternal life and will be provided with everything that is really important.

We will add two sections to this chapter suggesting one emphasis for a class where all, or most, are believing students and another for the opposite case.

D. Unconverted students

With this group it is worth noting that many did not accept with pleasure the provision made by God, nor do they all accept it today. God sent a perfect meal from heaven for the Israelites, but they despised it. God has given us the best He had in heaven, His beloved Son. To him who despises the Son of God and the salvation provided by him, damnation awaits. How shall we escape, if we neglect so great a salvation? 4

The conversation may extend to other portions of Scripture such as the following: Bread of nobles did man eat. 5 Our soul is dried up, for nothing but this manna is seen by our eyes. 6 Our soul is weary of this light bread. 7

The teacher's questions could be about the sufficiency of the manna and the attitude of the people, and should serve to emphasize the application of John 6:35, that Jesus Christ is the Bread of Life.

Well, let's now think of an illustration of our own for this class. Here in Venezuela, a group of doctors conducted an investigation into malnutrition among young children in the country. They discovered that many children suffered from rickets because they did not drink milk. But this was not so much because there was no milk, but because they did not like it, they did not like to drink it. The Israelite who willfully despised the manna, a food that had all the vitamins and proteins necessary for the health of the body, had to pay dearly for the consequences. In the same way, the unconverted young man who prefers television to the Word of God, the movies to the preaching cult and the world to Jesus Christ runs a serious risk of losing his soul. He

who refuses to eat the Bread of Life, that is, to believe in the Son of
God, will not see life, but the wrath of God is upon him. 8

E. Believing students

If the teacher limits his reading to Exodus 16, he will not be able to present everything concerning the subject of the manna. We have seen that there are other portions that abound in explanations for the unsaved; there are still more for God's people.

For the believer, eating the manna symbolizes meditating on the earthly life of humiliation of our Lord Jesus Christ. We partake of him to obtain salvation, according to John 6:54, but to receive sustenance in the spiritual life we must eat his flesh (6:56-58), meditating on his humiliation. By thus feeding ourselves daily we receive strength through his life.

The manna kept in an urn in the most holy place would be as a testimony for the descendants of the Israelites. We can discuss in class Exodus 16:33 and Hebrews 9:4, coming to verse 23 where it speaks of figures of heavenly things. The hidden manna makes us think of the exaltation of the Lord. Revelation 2:17 speaks of manna for the overcomer. The study could deal first with the manna scattered for salvation and then with the hidden manna received by the believer who overcomes in the trial. A discussion of the trials in the Christian life and the importance of being an overcomer in them will not interest the younger students or the unsaved, but will be very appropriate for a class of believers.

Finally we can mention Joshua 5:12, where it says that the manna ceased. The manna was for the wilderness but in the promised land there were better delicacies. The Lord has given us ample provision for this life, but better things lie ahead. We must eat of it here, seeking daily what has been provided for the journey, but in heaven the provisions of earthly life will not be needed because we will have entered into eternal rest.

In your Word, O Father God, What beautiful light is seen!

Blessed, heavenly portion enjoyed by faith.

9. INTRODUCING THE CLASS

The teacher who arrives to Sunday School early will have more time to arrange the material to be used in the lesson presentation, draw a map, or write an outline on the blackboard. In addition, you will be able to greet students as they arrive and sit with them. This personal attention is welcomed by the children and youth.

The time the teacher has with his class is relatively little. He must make the best use of it. Remember that of the 168 hours in a week, only one hour is shared with the class!

A. Opening

In some Sunday Schools the opening is done when all or several of the classes are together. Here we will deal with the opening in the particular class of each teacher. It is good to begin with a prayer asking for the Lord's help. The prayer before the students should be brief. Long prayers are for when we are alone with the Lord. At the beginning of the class it is appropriate to welcome new students.

B. Recitation

Students quote the verses they have learned by heart during the week. To save time in a large class, early arrivals can recite their texts to the teacher before the opening. Each student should have his or her verse sheet or notebook, although learning verses directly from the Bible may be appropriate for older students.

We know that it is important to memorize the Scriptures, but the teacher must be concerned that his disciples understand the truths of the subject so that they can express the thoughts in their own words. The student who understands the Scriptures is making progress, but our goal is for the student to apply the Word of God to his own life. Paul wrote to Timothy, "The Holy Scriptures are able to make you wise to salvation through faith which is in Christ Jesus." 1 The prophet Micah says of God, Do not my words do good to him that walketh uprightly? 2

C. Review

The purpose of true study is not merely to know, but to be able to apply the knowledge. Only frequent review can give this mastery of the truths taught. A review is more than repetition because it must shed new light on the lesson and confirm the application.

At the beginning of each lesson we briefly review the previous lesson. New questions will lead the students to more interest in the material already studied. The review at the beginning can serve as an introduction to the new lesson. The rule of teaching according to Isaiah 28 is: Commandment upon commandment, commandment upon commandment, line upon line.

D. Reading of the Word of God

Encourage students to bring their Bibles to class and take part in the reading. If the teacher asks questions about the passage before the reading they will pay more attention, looking for the answers as they read the portion. The Bible is the only book that should be read during class time. The teacher who prepares his lesson well will not read the teacher's manual or any other book in front of the class. Our only text is the Word of God.

E. Introduction

By means of a good introduction we awaken interest in the subject we propose to teach. Before we start teaching a subject that will take several weeks, we should present in an interesting way a summary of our plan. If the students know what the objectives of the teaching are, they will be more interested in the lessons. A sense of purpose helps in learning and the feeling of accomplishment of the purpose stimulates the students.

There are many ways to introduce a lesson. For example: relate something extraordinary that happened recently, draw a scene on the board, refer to the experiences of a child in the class, show an object or picture, ask an attention-getting question, refer to a question a student has asked, review the previous week's story, listen to a report a student has prepared, etc.

F. Teaching the lesson

The task of the educator is to awaken and put into action the mind of the disciple. Many times we err in trying to teach the lesson by means of the simple spoken word. Knowledge does not always pass from one mind to another by mere speech. We have to stimulate the student to acquire knowledge by discovering truths for himself.

How can we do this? Here are some activities for students: Bringing the Bible to class and looking up answers in it in verses quoted by the teacher; marking the Bible carefully under the direction of the instructor; preparing and presenting as homework reports on biblical characters or places; drawing maps by tracing on them routes and distances; singing a hymn or chorus expressing the theme of the lesson (this will be done if it is possible to do so without disturbing the other classes); drawing illustrations representing biblical truths (students may bring pencil and notebook to do these works at the end of class, as a review). These activities are intended to fix the knowledge in the mind and heart of each student.

How many truths should we teach the child in each lesson? Instead of trying to teach seven truths in one hour it is better to teach only one, perhaps doing it in seven different ways.

The students are the object of our first consideration. Each one of them has to participate in the classroom activities and learn. It is not the same to tell something as to teach it. We have to find out what the students do not know, then make up for what they lack, and then see if they have actually understood what they have been taught.

G. Teacher's questions

Our duty as teachers is to awaken the minds of the pupils and not rest until the child shows mental activity, gives his opinion and acts in class. Let us restrain our impatience. Let the student explain himself. Do not interrupt him or put words in his mouth. *How?* and *why?* questions make the child think more than questions about *what, who,* and *where.*

If someone gives a wrong answer, instead of saying *No!* and giving the correct answer, it is better to rephrase the question in a way that is easier to understand. If part of the answer is correct, let's approve that part and then explain the teaching better. We must prevent the student who answered wrong from feeling sorry and stop answering in class.

One method that the teacher will find effective is to direct questions to the whole class, to get everyone thinking, and then to name the students, one at a time, so that everyone gives their answer. The teacher hears the answers without nodding to the one who answers correctly, since by asking the next person, the next person would already know that the question has been answered. We must also teach the children to respect the opinions of their classmates and avoid teasing them when they hear a wrong answer.

There are many uses we can make of questions. Here are some examples:

1. Introduce a subject. The Lord Jesus did this by asking: "Who do men say that the Son of Man is the Son of Man? 3

2. Demand an explanation. Christ demanded of those who criticized him: Is it lawful on the sabbath days to do good? 4 How could they say no?

3. Asking the opinion of a student. By saying: What do you think, Simon? 5 the Lord awakened his disciple's interest in the explanation he was about to give.

4. Guide the child to apply the truth of the lesson. After having told the parable of the Good Samaritan, the Lord Jesus applied the parable to his listeners by asking: Which of these three seems to have been the neighbor? 6

H. Student questions

Teach students to ask questions. The narrative should not exhaust the subject, but we should leave something unsaid, to stimulate students' thinking and effort. Let's get the students to ask questions, leaving them time to think. It is better not to answer promptly the questions they ask, but to wait a moment to give them more strength. Whenever possible, it is good to respond with new questions, which will deepen the thinking. Jesus Christ often answered questions with questions. The Pharisees asked: Why do your disciples break the tradition of the elders? Christ said: Why do you also break the commandment of God with your tradition? 7

In the Old Testament we find several times the phrase: When thy son asketh. 8 Undoubtedly, the Israelite was obliged to answer his son with the Word of God. How important it is that we, the teachers, know how to answer the questions of our disciples!

A young man, attending Sunday School for the first time, heard the story of Elijah on Mount Carmel. 9 The boy asked the teacher, If it didn't rain for three years and six months, where did they get twelve pitchers of water? The teacher, a little irritated, replied, "God was able to provide the water. The boy felt sorry and never returned to class.

A few years passed and this boy heard the preaching of the gospel and was saved. One day, looking at a map in his Bible, he noticed that Mount Carmel was near the sea. He remembered his question and thought: If the teacher had told me that they could have used salt water from the sea to wet the altar, perhaps I would have continued to attend his class.

From the use of questions arises discussion, which is a form of participation on the part of the students. Discussion allows almost everyone to participate. In this way some individuals feel free to express themselves. If we encourage questions we will keep the way open for students to contribute their knowledge.

I. Teacher's language

———

Let us try to teach the gospel using understandable words that are part of the student's vocabulary. There are biblical words that require explanation such as: spare, atone, justify, reconcile, redeem, and remit, to name a few.

The teacher can use symbolic language, but it is necessary to explain what is being referred to. For example, if he speaks of black and white hearts, he should clarify that he is not referring to the physical organ, nor to the color of the skin, but to the inner being. 10 The black represents the contamination of sin and the white speaks of the cleansing that provides salvation. 12

It is biblical to speak of the glory of the Lord, as when John writes: We saw his glory, glory as of the only begotten of the Father. 13 But some children think this refers to a halo that was seen above his head or a light that surrounded him. It is rather about his character. The divine glory of the Lord Jesus was revealed in every detail of His earthly life.

Another term that requires explanation is *the law*. The teacher knows that it refers to the commandments that God gave to Israel, 14 but many students have only heard of the labor law or the traffic law.

Some talk a lot about sin when students do not understand what the word means. Sin includes evil thoughts, 15 deceit, bad temper, lying, 16 evil words, and pride. Also to him that knoweth to do good, and doeth it not, to him it is sin. 17

To young children, it is better not to tell them that they are going to hell, but we should explain to them what separation from God means as a consequence of sin. 18 To those who, because of their age, are already responsible before God, we must teach them what Christ taught 19 and what other Scriptures say about hell, 20 where all those who reject Christ and his salvation will go.

It is unfortunate that many times biblical truths are falsified or taken in the wrong sense because they appear in expressions that are not understood. That is why we must:

Pay attention to the language of the students, in order to know the words they use and the meaning they give to them.

2. To express ourselves, as far as possible, in the language of our students.

3. Use few words.

4. Clarify the meaning of new words, using illustrations for this purpose. When it is necessary to teach a new word, it is good to express the idea behind it before pronouncing the word.

5. To find out by means of questions the interpretation that the students give to the biblical words they learn, to ensure that they have the correct meaning of them.

J. Illustrations

Let us try to illustrate our lessons wisely. We should note that a joke is not an illustration. Here are some suggestions in this regard:

Use only illustrations that have to do with the truth we want to teach in the lesson.

2. Use true illustrations. If we use anecdotes or fables we must explain to the students their origin.

3. Know the data of the illustration well and give them in order.

Tell the story of the illustration in a simple, clear and interesting way.

5. Avoid making use of illustrations that praise ourselves. The humble worker does not use them.

K. Pictures, flannelgraphs and objects

A certain teacher said that he did not see the need to use this type of material in his class. For him it was enough to read and explain the Word of God. But, it seemed that he never realized that the only students who continued to attend were those who were forced to do so by believing parents.

We have the duty to maintain the interest of the students because without interest the student learns little or nothing. But it is better not to use what can divert us from the Word of God, because it is the Word that gives life. 21

When showing pictures it is good to explain to the children that this is how the artists painted them, but we do not really know what the Bible characters looked like physically. If the class is large we will not show small pictures in books because it is difficult for all the children to see the picture well.

Certain flannelgraph lessons are very useful in teaching children. If we are going to use a flannelgraph, it is advisable to study the lesson carefully and rehearse it at home, perhaps in front of a mirror.

The teacher can also use simple objects such as a flag, coins, a mirror, etc., to better teach the Scriptures. When using visual objects in a class we should avoid spending too much time with them, time that could be better spent with the Word itself. With care and experience, objects can bring out the Bible's own teaching.

Let's think of a lesson on the resurrection of believers at the coming of the Lord. We can use a magnet and some nails placed in some sand. When a student brings the magnet close to the sand, the iron nails will go up, and the copper or other metal nails will stay where the teacher put them. When Christ comes into the air, the dead believers will come up, and the living also. 22 Those who died without Christ will remain in their graves until the second resurrection. 23 Thus we see how the teacher can make his explanation of spiritual things clearer without resorting to costly devices or complex techniques that rob the place that the reading of the Holy Scriptures should occupy.

L. Hymns and choruses

Let us try to teach the hymns that express the Gospel. Sometimes it is necessary to explain the meaning of some expressions in the hymns so that the students sing with understanding.

We have suggested that the class sing certain hymns according to the theme of the lesson, but in many schools the groups are all in the same room or the divisions are very thin and the class cannot sing without getting in the way of the others. If singing is possible, fine; but if it is not possible, quoting the words of a well-known hymn or chorus can support the teaching of the subject even if it cannot be sung.

Lead me, O Lord, and I will guide the poor wanderer who goes so far away:

Give me food, and I also will give to the poor hungry man thy manna.

10. CLASSROOM DISCIPLINE
Causes of disorder

Lack of discipline greatly hinders teaching. If there is such a problem in our class we must determine the causes of the misbehavior and try to correct them.

It may be because the children are too crowded, it is too noisy outside, it is too hot and there is poor ventilation in the room. If it is just one child, perhaps he is misbehaving because he has problems at home or is suffering from an illness. If so, there is nothing to be gained by scolding. If we are unaware of their conflicts and concerns, we are at fault.

Many times, or most of the time, the lack of good order is due to the fact that we teachers do not give respect to our students. This may be our own fault. Perhaps we are not prepared to teach, we lack a vocation, or we are not kind or encouraging; perhaps the students perceive in us a lack of sincerity or carelessness in our preparation of the class.

Most Sunday School attendees go willingly. Some believers make great efforts to invite young people and children to Sunday School. But if there is noise and disorder in the class, the visiting student will not find the atmosphere pleasant and will not feel like attending. The apostle Paul wrote to the saints in Colossae: I am ... rejoicing and beholding your good order. 1 Could this be said of us, in the way we conduct the class that the Lord has entrusted to us?

Suggestions

The following suggestions may be helpful in solving some discipline problems: Students should be seated where they can see the teacher. There should be nothing behind the teacher to distract. From the beginning we must demand obedience and cooperation from everyone. If a boy is talking or getting in the way, stop talking and look him in the face until he understands the need to respect order. We are wasting our time if we continue to talk, pray or read while there is disorder. Sometimes it is possible to get a difficult child to cooperate by giving him a special task. If he does it well, we can praise him and thus gain his appreciation. The naughty child usually behaves better if he is sitting near his teacher.

It is necessary to prepare the lesson in such a way that there is enough activity for the whole class hour. This preparation requires diligence because some students are more capable than others and finish the work first. Every child must be busy at all times.

There are many ways to capture the interest of holding the learner's attention. The child can see, feel, hear, smell and taste, so we can reach his mind through any of his five senses. There are many objects that can be used in the classroom to make teaching clearer and more interesting. In addition, the smile, the movement of the hands, and the variation in the tone of the voice should accompany the words we pronounce in the class presentation.

It is necessary to speak in a clear and intelligible voice, but if we speak too loudly we disturb the other classes. The lesson will be more interesting if we proceed quickly at times. For example, we can tell the story of Zacchaeus 2 quickly, but when speaking of the sufferings of Jesus Christ we will speak slowly and reverently. After applying a solemn truth, it is good to pause so that the students take to heart what they have heard. We must imitate the readers of the time of Nehemiah who read in the book of the law of God clearly, and put the sense, so that they understood the reading. 3

The same routine every Sunday becomes monotonous for the child. To avoid this, we can vary our approach to the lesson from time to time. For example, we can leave the Scripture reading for the end and start with a memorized verse quiz. Without interest there is no good behavior and no learning.

What the disciple expects from the master

Love and understanding. The lost sheep in Matthew 18:12 is apparently a child, for these verses are part of the teaching that the Lord Jesus gave concerning children. Each child is different and some are kinder than others. We should never show favoritism towards some but love them all equally. Let us try not to scold but praise those who are well behaved and those who make an effort to learn the Word of God, encouraging them to behave even better. The Lord said: See that you do not despise one of these little ones. 4

2. Encouragement for the believing student. In the same chapter 18 of Matthew, the Lord speaks of the sin of causing one of these little ones who believe in him to stumble. Without realizing it, we could be guilty of that sin, either by discouraging a saved child by saying that he is not, or by demanding that he behave like an adult believer.

3. Good example. It is the teacher's obligation to show a holy, righteous and blameless conduct as the apostle Paul teaches us. We cannot expect from the student what he does not see in ourselves. Respect is not achieved by saying: I am a teacher, respect me. We read in Titus 1:7 that it is necessary for the bishop to be blameless, ... not proud or wrathful ... but loving and self-controlled. The same qualities are necessary in a Sunday School teacher. The student will know when his teacher has them and will also know when he does not have them.

I must set an example, fulfill my vocation

, And my talents to dedicate to Christ in service.

11. OTHER TEACHER ACTIVITIES

We have considered how the teacher should prepare and present the lesson, maintain order in the classroom and show interest in each student. Now we want to suggest other activities that the teacher should develop.

A. Lead students in preaching worship.

If the students are of an age to be saved, it is the duty of the teacher to take an interest in their souls and to seek to bring them also to the gospel preaching service and to sit with them in the service. Many of those who accept Christ in evangelistic services are, or were, Sunday School students.

B. Handing out evangelical literature

The Sunday School student is a good means by which the church can introduce Bible literature into the homes of unconverted families. Many adults read with more interest than their children the tracts and booklets the children receive in their classes.

C. Taking the class on field trips

Children love an excursion or a walk. If we schedule an excursion, it is advisable to ask for the cooperation of other brothers to supervise the children, even if the group is small. The excursion, or the visit of the students to the teacher's house, gives the boy the opportunity to see his teacher, not as an instructor with a coat and tie on, but as a person.

D. Visiting homes

We teachers would do well to visit the students' homes and gain the sympathy of their families. One teacher told the superintendent that she couldn't stand Cristobal because he bothered the other boys so much. The brother advised the teacher to visit the home. At Cristobal's home there were problems: the father had left home and the poor mother felt unable to raise her children. The teacher took Christopher and his sister into her home occasionally and cared for them as she cared for her children. Later that mother attended services and was converted.

E. Maintain contact with students from previous years

Let's try to maintain contact with students who have moved away or have stopped attending Sunday School for some other reason. A letter with a tract inside or a visit and invitation to preaching services can bring good results.

F. Prepare and present programs

It is the custom in many Sunday Schools to hold an annual special meeting for the students. On these occasions one brother addresses the students and another may speak to the parents. The teachers give out prizes to the students who have been punctual and diligent during the year. A program presented by the students is part of this meeting.

This program has several objectives: to stimulate students to learn and quote the Scriptures well; to teach them to sing hymns; to present the gospel to the public; to encourage parents to attend worship services; to encourage parents to send their children to Bible classes; to encourage parents to help their children learn the Word.

Many parents attend these meetings because they want to see their children perform in front of an audience; therefore, in view of the objectives already mentioned, it is desirable that every student take part in the program. Let us take care that the program does not run too long. To save time, children can go on the platform class by class or in large groups. Each student who is able to do so can recite a verse or part of a verse aloud. It is good if all the verses recited by the group are related to each other. Then the students will sing a hymn or chorus related to the theme in question. The themes should be based on the Gospel. For example: The birth of the Savior, 1 Jesus Christ; the door of salvation; 2 the invitation of the gospel (verses and hymns that express invitation). It is desirable that the theme be one that the class has studied during the year.

It is not advisable for teachers to spend months rehearsing the program with their students. In view of how much of God's Word they will want to teach over the course of the year, six weeks will be sufficient time to prepare the program. It is preferable to bring the students together during the week, perhaps at the teacher's home, to learn hymns. It is good to practice the program at least once as it will be presented so that the children learn to get on and off the platform.

In some Sunday Schools the children of believing parents or some who have special abilities participate several times in the program. This does not give other children the opportunity to participate. The program would fulfill its objective if all students are encouraged, if unconverted families hear the gospel and if the name of the Lord is glorified.

G. Pray intelligently for each member of the class.

It is a common thing for the teacher or superintendent to keep a notebook in the classroom with the names of the students, their attendance points and addresses, ages, grade levels, etc., at hand. But teachers truly consecrated to the Lord and to the work He has entrusted to them keep a second notebook at home and use it in their private prayer. This contains the list of their students and certain data about them, such as the attitude of their families to the gospel, the desires and doubts the young person has expressed to the teacher, etc. If the class is passed on to another teacher, all or part of this information may be passed on to him.

H. Self-examination

A s teachers we examine our disciples from time to time. Why not examine ourselves? The duty of every believer is to test himself. 3 We can ask ourselves:

1. Do I long for the salvation of my students?

2. Am I enjoying the presence and help of the Lord, or am I relying on my own talents and abilities?

3. What motivates me? Is it a worthy motive?

Am I a better teacher than last year or am I going backwards?

A heart of love, I want Jesus, to be like you, Lord, full of light

; So may I serve, time redeem, and souls direct, Lord, to thee.

12. RESULTS
We want to avoid false professions

Much attendance and interest are good and desirable things, but we are not going to be satisfied with this. We must examine, in the light of God's Word, our lack of success in the Lord's work. In this way we will be able to correct our mistakes and bear more fruit for the Lord.

Some teachers become discouraged when students profess to be saved and then show by their deeds that they are not. In the parable of the Sower in Matthew 13 the Lord spoke of the seed that sprouted but then withered because it had no root, and of another part that was choked by thorns.

Two great causes of false professions are: lack of knowledge of the Gospel by those who profess to be saved and lack of dependence on the Holy Spirit by those who evangelize. To tell an individual that he must believe in the Lord Jesus Christ when he does not yet appreciate the work and person of the Lord is to invite the blind man's question: Who is he, Lord, that I should believe in him? 1

We want genuine results

—

Christ must be presented before inviting a person to trust in him. The apostle John wrote his gospel: That you may believe that Jesus is the Christ, the Son of God, and that believing you may have life in his name. 2 John begins his book by presenting the deity of the Lord and his manifestation in flesh, full of grace and truth. 3 He goes on to mention seven times when the Lord speaks of himself saying: I am ... After highlighting excellencies of his character he describes in detail the events of the death, burial and resurrection of the Lord Jesus Christ.

Thus the spiritual teacher seeks to present the Lord Jesus in such a way that the disciple has a true appreciation of him. Paul affirmed: We preach Christ crucified, 4 and summarized his teaching of the Gospel in three truths: That Christ died for our sins ... that he was buried, and that he rose again the third day, according to the Scriptures. 5

But even when we have tried to declare the whole counsel of God, we must keep in mind that the work of salvation is of the Spirit. In our desire for results we must never seek to do on our own what is the exclusive work of the Holy Spirit.

It is true that the student has to choose, but a decision is not a conversion to God. Moreover, it is a great mistake to tell a person that he is saved if he believes such and such a verse, without first recognizing his sinful state and the danger in which he finds himself. This must come before he feels the need to trust wholeheartedly in the person and work of the Savior. We read this in the Gospels. Many believed in his name, seeing the signs he did. But Jesus Himself did not trust them because He knew everyone, and had no need for anyone to testify to Him about the man, for He knew what was in the man. 7

How can we obtain genuine results?

1. We must pray for the Spirit to do His work. Not by might, nor by power, but by my Spirit, says the LORD. 3 The results of the Spirit's work are spontaneous. After the preaching on the day of Pentecost, it was not the preachers who came to the hearers, but those who heard, who were of good heart, who said to Peter and to the other apostles, Men and brethren, what shall we do? 9

2. We must keep in mind that the faith of those who seek salvation must be based on *faith*. By this we mean the Word of God. God's truth is the only foundation. If we are truly convinced of this, such conviction will have a great influence on the way we conduct ourselves in the class under our care.

Wisdom is required with the student who has made a profession of faith in the Lord Jesus. If the child or young person has believed it is good to encourage him to act. Conversion is the first step, not the last. From then on the pupil should seek with the Lord's help to give up bad habits. Even a child can testify of the great things the Lord has done with him. 10 The wise believer will not disregard the child who has confessed the name of the Lord, but neither will he harm him by pushing him beyond what he has learned by self-exercise.

4. Our objective will not only be to see the students saved but baptized, 11 gathered in the name of the Lord, 12 worshiping and serving Him.

In Jehovah is the strength 13

Sometimes the teacher feels cold and discouraged. The cause may be difficulties in the family or at work, illness, or neglect of the spiritual. If there is neglect we must seek the presence of God and confess our sin.

If we want to be faithful in the ministry of teaching we must ignore the difficulties. Paul encourages us with his example when he says: "I do not pay attention to anything. 14 On many occasions David was a prey to trouble ... but he strengthened himself in the LORD his God. 15

Salvation is of Jehovah 16

One believer had accepted the Lord at an advanced age. He never felt qualified to take a public part in the large church of which he was a member. However, he took charge of a ward Sunday School class, befriending the youth group assigned to him.

Years later a man came to the door of that master's house. An old woman opened the door and when the man asked about her teacher she said, "My husband died recently.

-Oh," said the visitor, "I was a student in a Bible class where he taught, and I have never forgotten his words. I came to tell him that the day before yesterday I was saved.

Cast thy bread upon the waters, for after many days thou shalt find it. 17

Jochebed, Moses' mother, took the child from the hands of Pharaoh's daughter and raised him. Later she had to give the child to the princess, and Moses spent many years in the royal palace. 19 But what he had learned about the God of his fathers bore fruit in due time, for as a great man Moses chose the reproach of Christ rather than the treasures of the Egyptians; for he had his eye on the reward. 20 Many times the results are not seen immediately, for that reason the teacher should not be discouraged. God can keep the seed sown.

But, of course, the work will be in vain if we stop watering the seed with our prayers. We have to spend more time talking to God about the students than talking to the students about God.

A sister taught Sunday morning classes after the Lord's Supper. She had a desire to do something else. As she read Ecclesiastes 11:6, "In the morning sow your seed, and in the evening do not let your hand rest; for you do not know which is best," she thought she could teach a class in a ward Bible school on Sunday afternoons. The Lord blessed her double effort.

We may feel our weakness and lack of faithfulness, but the message is greater than the messenger. We have a great responsibility but at the same time a great privilege. Ours is the opportunity to win souls and guide young lives in the ways of the Lord. With the serious dedication that this work demands, and with prayer, perseverance and faith, we may in time see some results of our efforts that will be to the glory of God.

Servants of God, pray! There is still much to do;

Proclaim the good news to children everywhere.

BIBLICAL REFERENCES

CHAPTER 1

———

Matthew 11:25

Matthew 18:1-5

Luke 18:16

John 21:15

Matthew 21:16

6. Mark 6:34

CHAPTER 2

Matthew 15:14

2. 1 Corinthians 2:14

3. 2 Timothy 2:15

4. 1 Thessalonians 2:10

5. 2 Corinthians 5:14

Colossians 3:23

7. 2 Timothy 1:6

John 16:13

James 5:16

10. 1 Timothy 4:13

Ephesians 5:25

CHAPTER 3

Ephesians 1:6

2. Ecclesiastes 11 :9

3. Ecclesiastes 12:1

CHAPTER 4

Luke 24:27

Genesis 22

Genesis 45:7

John 3:14, 15

Exodus 35:10-19

Genesis 3

Genesis 18 and 19

Genesis 22

Genesis 24

Genesis 44 and 45

Exodus 12

Leviticus 16

Numbers 21

Joshua 2 and 6

Ezekiel 37

16. Romans 8:1

17. Romans 7:18

18. 1 Thessalonians 4:13

19. 2 Corinthians 5:10 and

1 Corinthians 3:13-15

CHAPTER 5

Matthew 23:8

Job 36:22

John 7:46

Matthew 13:54

Acts 1:1

Luke 24:19

7. Amos 7:8

Jeremiah 24:2

Jeremiah 1:11

Jeremiah 13:7

Matthew 22:19

12. Matthew 6:26

Matthew 6:28

14. Mark 9:36

John 13:4

16. John 6:11

Matthew 7:15

John 12:24

Matthew 23:27

John 3:8

Matthew 16:13

22. Mark 3:4

Matthew 17:25

24. Luke 10:36

25. Hosea 12:10

Judges 9:8

27. 2 Samuel 12:1

Matthew 13:34

29. Luke 15:11

30. Luke 15

31. Luke 7:32

32. Luke 10:25

Matthew 22:11

John 3

35. John 6:63

CHAPTER 6

Judges 6:11

Luke 16:8

Jeremiah 48:10

Proverbs 4:23

John 5:39

Philippians 4:9

7. 1 Timothy 4:13

Colossians 3:23

9. Ecclesiastes 12:9

Hebrews 11:16

CHAPTER 7

Luke 7:14

2. 1 Corinthians 13:11

Romans 5:12

4. 2 Timothy 3:15

Deuteronomy 6:6

Matthew 5 - 7

CHAPTER 8

1. Ecclesiastes 12:1

2. Proverbs 8:17

Nehemiah 9:21

Hebrews 2:3

Psalm 78:25

Numbers 11:6

Numbers 21:5

John 3:36

CHAPTER 9

1. 2 Timothy 3:15

2. Micah 2:7

Matthew 16:13

4. Mark 3:4

Matthew 17:25

Luke 10:36

Matthew 15.2,3

Exodus 13:14,

Deuteronomy 6:20, Joshua 4:6

9. 1 Kings 18:34

10. Jeremiah 17:9, Psalm 51:10

Jeremiah 2:22

Psalm 51:7

13. John 1:14

Leviticus 26:46

15. Mark 7:21

Revelation 21:8

17. James 4:17

John 8:21

19. Luke 16:23 and Matthew 8:12

20. Revelation 14:11 and Jude 13

21. John 6:63

22. 1 Thessalonians 4:16,17

Revelation 12-15

CHAPTER 10

Colossians 2:5

2. Luke 19:1

Nehemiah 8:8

Matthew 18:10

5. 1 Thessalonians 2:10

CHAPTER 11

Matthew 1, Luke 1 and 2 John 10

3. 1 Corinthians 11:28

CHAPTER 12

1. John 9:36

John 20:31

John 1:14

4. 1 Corinthians 1:23

5. 1 Corinthians 15:1-4

6. Acts 20:27

John 2:23-25

Zechariah 4:6

9. Acts 2:37

Psalm 126:3

11. Acts 2:41

12. Matthew 18:20,

1 Corinthians 11:23-26

Isaiah 26:4

14 Acts 20:24

15. I Samuel 30:6

Jonah 2.9

17. Ecclesiastes 11:1

Exodus 6.20

Exodus 2:10

Hebrews 11:26

Don't miss out!

Visit the website below and you can sign up to receive emails whenever Bible Sermons publishes a new book. There's no charge and no obligation.

https://books2read.com/r/B-A-MZBS-DKVBD

BOOKS 2 READ

Connecting independent readers to independent writers.

Did you love *How to Teach in Sunday School: A Guide for Bible Class Teachers*? Then you should read *Analyzing Labor Education in Matthew's Gospel*[1] by Bible Sermons!

[2]

From Matthew's Gospel we can learn several important lessons about work education:

1. work with dedication and responsibility: Jesus praised the faithful servants who multiplied the talents entrusted to them. This teaches us the importance of working diligently and responsibly in our tasks and responsibilities.

2. Be wise stewards: In the parable of the talents, Jesus teaches the importance of being good stewards of the resources we have been given. This involves using **our gifts and abilities for the benefit of others and for the fulfillment of God's purposes.**

---

1. https://books2read.com/u/merwOZ

2. https://books2read.com/u/merwOZ

3. Seek God's kingdom first: Jesus taught his followers to seek first the kingdom of God and his righteousness, trusting that God will provide all that is needed. This implies prioritizing our relationship with God and his will over our personal goals and ambitions.

4. Be diligent in God's work: Jesus instructed his disciples to proclaim the gospel and make disciples of all nations. *This teaches us the importance of being diligent in God's work and fulfilling the calling He has given us.*

Also by Bible Sermons

A Collection of Biblical Sermons
The Power of Great Gospel Words
The Power of Prayer: Men Ought Always to Pray
The Power of the Single Life in Christ
Analyzing The Power of a Life in Christ

Bible Characters Collection
Analyzing Biblical Scenes: 62 Inspiring Christian Teachings from the
Old Testament

Notes in the New Testament
Analyzing Notes in the Book of Matthew: Fulfillments of Old
Testament Prophecies
Analyzing Notes in the Book of Mark: Finding Peace in Difficult
Times
Analyzing Notes in the Book of Luke: The Divine Love of Jesus
Revealed
Analyzing Notes in the Book of John: John's Contribution to the New
Testament Scriptures

Analyzing Notes in the Book of the Acts of the Apostles: A Journey of Continuation in the Work of Jesus

Overflying The Bible
Symbols in the Bible: Healthy Christian Doctrine
Bible Introduction: Overflying The Bible from Genesis by Brethren in the Faith
Chronological Prophecy: Things That Will Happen on Earth
Bible Study: Genesis 1. Creation in Six Days

Teaching in the Bible class
Sunday School Lessons: 182 Bible Stories
Bible Class for Beginners: 50 Beautiful Lessons
Lessons for Sunday School: 62 Biblical Characters
How to Teach in Sunday School: A Guide for Bible Class Teachers

Teaching in the Bible Classroom
Studying Teaching in the Bible Classroom: A Teacher's Guide

The Education of Labor in the Bible
Analyzing the Education of Labor in Genesis: The Purpose of Life on Earth
Analyzing the Teaching of Labor in Exodus: From Slavery to Liberation
Analyzing the Labor Education in Leviticus: The Spirit of the Law at Work

Standalone

About the Author

This bible study series is perfect for Christians of any level, from children to youth to adults. It provides an engaging and interactive way to learn the Bible, with activities and discussion topics that will help deepen your understanding of scripture and strengthen your faith. Whether you're a beginner or an experienced Christian, this series will help you grow in your knowledge of the Bible and strengthen your relationship with God. Led by brothers with exemplary testimonies and extensive knowledge of scripture, who congregate in the name of the Lord Jesus Christ throughout the world.